The People's History

Geordie Muddling by Ripyard Cuddling

A Collection of Geordie Poems

by Jack Davitt

Grey's Monument – one of many famous Geordie landmarks.

Previous page: Ready for the tin bath – once a common site in many North East homes.

Copyright © Jack Davitt 2001

First published in 2001 by

The People's History Ltd
Suite 1
Byron House
Seaham Grange Business Park
Seaham
Co. Durham
SR7 0PY

ISBN 1 902527 76 3

Contents

Silly Dreams

The magic works of Wordsworth
Were born amid the Fells
Beside the Derwent Water
And the lovely Lakeland dells.

With this beauty all around him
Of sun blest hills and vale
Surrounded by this majesty
How could a poet fail?

On the western coast of Scotland
Where the ether tastes like wine
Where the heather bells are scattered
And the hills are clad with pine.

It was here a famous Scotsman
First saw the light of day
In a humble ploughman's cottage
At a place called Alloway

On the edge of 'God's own country'
Where the kestrel wheels and turns
The boy grew up to manhood
His name was 'Robbie Burns'.

Yes, Burns had Bonnie Scotland
And Wordsworth had the Lakes
And they'll never be forgotten
For they both had what it takes.

Their works will be remembered
Each verse and every line
Wordsworth for his 'Daffodils'
And Burns for 'Auld Lang Syne'.

I'm just a shipyard worker
No talents grand, have I
No Lakes have I to dream by
No kestrel in my sky.

My world is grimmer, bleaker
Not for the poet's pen
A world of noise and clamour
And sweating, cursing men.

Yet if a chance was given
A welcome change of view
And maybe just a touch of luck
I'd be a poet too.

Foreword

You might say I've known 'Cuddling' for years. Ever since the late 1970s, when I came across the rough typesheets of welder Jack Davitt's rhyming couplets being bandied around Swan Hunter's shipyard and the surrounding pubs and clubs by his workmates. As an 'Educated Geordie' myself, whose father had served as a fitter in the same shipyard, the whole idea of a working class bloke penning his verse between welds really appealed to me, as it no doubt would have done to the Newcastle writer, and mentor of mine, Jack Common.

And so it was time to seek out 'Ripyard Cuddling', alias Welder Jack, and make him an offer he couldn't refuse. A pint or three at the nearby 'Wheatsheaf' and I was knocking on his door. "How about a selection of your poems in a booklet?", I proffered – and the Bard of Holystone took no persuading. *Shipyard Muddling by Ripyard Cuddling* read the cover, with the witty sketches of my mate Julian Watson (alias 'Crawford Crowquill') adding to the wit of Jack's fertile pen. Soon it hit the shelves as part of the 'Strong Words' series of community publications intent on giving the ordinary people of the North East of England their say. And it sold like 'Fed Special' – over 3,000 copies, in fact, with a big splash in the national *Guardian* bringing the postie to my door with sackfuls of letters and orders from Geordies the World over. "A sequel!" the crowd bayed, and, before too long, out came *More Muddling by Cuddling*, another runaway success, this time illustrated by fellow shipyard man Peter Burns.

Now these wee booklets are available from North Tyneside Libraries, in association with my own imprint 'Northern Voices', in a combined edition, with a foreword by Tony Benn, one of Ripyard's greatest fans. All very well, but what we all cried out for was a broader collection, not just about the yards but also dealing with Jack the life and soul of West Allotment Club, his loves, his times, his beer. And so we have it, the definitive edition of the poems of a working class man of wit and generosity, brought together in this fine 'People's History' edition. I hope it goes like hot whippets and, as a local poet myself, I doff my cap to my mate Jack and trust that he'll be getting the first round in when next I share a few pints with him at the Club.

Cheers 'Cuddling' – and keep the pencil sharpened. In these often gloomy days, we need your warm humanity.

Keith Armstrong
Coordinator, 'Northern Voices'

I would like to dedicate this book to my daughter, Tricia.

Going for a stroll in Wallsend Park in the 1930s.

Acknowledgements

I owe any success I have in no small measure to Keith Armstrong and Frank Wappat, without them I would still be a secret poet.

I would also like to thank:

Tom Bainbridge, Ian S. Carr, Lily Groves, Evan Martin, George Nairn, Neil Taylor, Wallsend People's Centre, Billy Ward, Tony Whittle.

Produced in association with North Tyneside Libraries.

Jack's previous book, *Shipyard Muddling and More Muddling*, is available from North Tyneside Libraries.

THE INCOMPLETE POET

Jack Davitt – shipyard welder and poet.

The Incomplete Poet

I used to be a poet
At least that's what I thought
My ego was enormous
But my talents were too short.

I searched for inspiration
In every book I read
And clever words and phrases
Collided in my head.

To put these words on paper
Required skill and time
But I didn't have the 'Know how'
And I couldn't make them rhyme.

Did Shelley have these set backs?
When he applied the pen
Did Wordsworth and his daffodils
Have problems now and then?

If those poetic giants
Had problems such as these
Then what can be my chances?
A welder, if you please.

Shakespeare was a genius
A clever lad was Will
He gave us all those classic works
Armed only with a quill.

The undisputed champion
Of literary men
Imagine what he might have done
If he'd had a ball point pen.

I sadly turn the pages
My heart filled with despair
For I'll never be a Kipling
Or a Walter De La Mare.

That little bit of magic
That makes a poet tick
Is missing from my 'make up'
It's enough to make you sick.

I studied Kipling's verses
With envy and dismay
The works of Keats and Byron
And that 'Elegy' by Gray.

I reached the sad conclusion
That I could never win
So I gathered up my manuscripts
And threw them in the bin.

I carry in my pocket
The pen I used to wield
The pen that was my ally
In the literary field.

It's just a plastic 'Biro'
Reliable although
Like my papers and my manuscripts
My pen will have to go.

I'm looking for a 'Somewhere'
Where sadly I can throw it
I was pretty good at welding
But I'll never make a poet.

Jack – with pen in hand – writing a verse at his local club.

The Story Of A Geordie Poet
by Jack Davitt

It was on the 27th day of August in the year 1924 that I first saw the light of day. I was born in the little colliery village of Old Benton Square, the youngest of three brothers. The conditions in the village were primitive to say the least. We had no electricity and no plumbing, these luxuries were only for other people, not for mining families. My father worked hard down the pit to keep his wife and three sons, and looking back I can remember I had a very happy childhood. I started school at the age of five years but I'm afraid my scholastic career was not very successful. I found arithmetic to be an insurmountable problem, and history and geography were completely beyond me. However, my teacher told me that my understanding of English was quite acceptable, and my handwriting was quite up to standard.

As my schooldays advanced I took to writing stories and sometimes I made them rhyme. They weren't very good rhymes, but I was very proud of some of my work, and I became a sort of a secret poet. No one ever saw this early work of mine because I had a feeling that poetry would not go down very well with my 'football mad' school pals. A few years later, when I was eighteen and in the Royal Navy, I was doing a course on telegraphy when I wrote a poem about my classmates. I was quite proud of it and had it typed out and showed it to the other lads. It went down very well with them and I gained a reputation as being a 'bit of a poet'.

Old Benton Square, circa 1910.

Come the end of the war, I was demobbed, and returned to the shipyard to finish my interrupted apprenticeship as a welder. Travelling to work as an apprentice welder proved to be very difficult as there was no direct bus to Wallsend. I had to walk about a mile to the Wallsend road junction in order to catch a bus. If I missed this bus then that was a shift lost, as there was only one bus per day. So I decided to get myself a push bike as cheaply as possible. I remember the back mudguard was missing and the front mudguard was fastened up with string. The bike had a distinctive rattle and on pressing the left hand pedal it gave a loud squeak in the key of 'C'. The right hand pedal gave a corresponding squeak in the key of 'G' and thus equipped I would proceed down Station Road for all the world like a one man band. This was how I became famous as the 7.15 am travelling alarm clock.

I made some very good friends in the shipyards and I worked in quite a few of them. I worked in the Hebburn Yard of Leslie, the Walker Naval Yard and the Neptune Yard before returning to the Wallsend Shipyard, where I finished off my working days. I have some very happy memories of my days in the shipyards, many of which I have tried to capture in verse. I said I have some happy memories of the shipyards, but it would be true to say I also have some very unhappy memories of them. Sometimes I have nightmares remembering the

Jack in the Royal Navy during the Second World War.

conditions that we often had to work in. Memories of tanks full of welding fumes where we had to do piece work for eight hour shifts and the harder we worked, the more we added to the fumes. The mind penetrating noise of the caulking machines and sparks from the burners would descend on you like a white hot shower of molten snow flakes. However, those of us who weren't choked by the fumes, or deafened by the noise or burnt to death by the sparks managed to keep our sense of humour, it was a case of keep smiling or find yourself another job. But strangely there were very few who deserted the shipyard until fate stepped in and closed them down.

Ninety percent of shipyard workers enjoyed a pint of ale and most of that ninety percent were members of a social club. I remember during the dinner break when the Coronation Club was crammed wall to wall with thirsty Swan Hunter's men who consumed their daily 'pint and pie'. For a brief hour the fumes and the noise and dreaded burners' sparks were forgotten. I have to admit that this break was the highlight of my day and I would return to my welding duties in the gloomy tanks refreshed and recharged. The club has always played a big part of my life and the weekends have always found me in my own local club at West Allotment. I have been a member there for more years than I care to remember, and one can always find good company, a good pint and a good 'crack' there.

The year 1958 proved to be a landmark year in my career. I was now a fully fledged welder. I had been married for eleven years to Margaret – we were blessed with three children, two sons and a daughter – and in all the years we have been together she has been my anchor and my best friend. This was the year I started work at Walker Naval Yard and this was the year when I got really bitten by the poetry bug. An amateur poet like me couldn't go wrong with all the material that was

Daughter, Tricia with granddaughter, Tina. Tina holds up her certificate for winning the Butlins Holiday Princess Competition.

at hand in the Naval Yard. The yard was full of some of the most interesting and entertaining characters I have ever met, and I tried my best to put some of their amusing escapades into verse. They were written in long hand on every scrap of paper that was available. One of my workmates – Peter McKenna – insisted he took some of my verse home where his daughter typed them out on foolscap. Somehow or other these poems found their way into the office upstairs, there they were photocopied and distributed among the Naval Yard workforce. I expected to be reprimanded by the management, but my luck held and I got off Scot-free. I stayed at the Naval Yard for eight years during which time I managed to compose quite a large number of what I like to think were poems, many of them, alas, have gone astray. My stay at the Naval Yard was coming to an end, the work programme was beginning to falter so I applied for a job back at my home yard at Wallsend.

My wife, Margaret, had a similar background to me, she came from the colliery village of West Moor, which was situated about two miles from Old Benton Square. She had a very close friend – Elsie – and the two of them had always been together from being toddlers and many people mistakenly took them for sisters. In later life, Elsie was to marry a good friend of mine, his name was Reyner. The four of us became

Jack's wife, Margaret (left) with friends Elsie and Reyner.

inseparable and everything we did, we did together. Elsie was very talented and one of the wittiest people I have ever known – she was always the life and soul of the party. She sometimes used to write little snippets of rhyme and she always used to sign them with the pen name 'Ripyard Cuddling'. I used to think that was a hilarious non-de-plume and in 1958, when I took my first faltering steps into the world of poetry, I asked her permission if I could steal it. She agreed of course, and so I became 'Ripyard Cuddling Mark Two'. Elsie and Reyner have both passed away and are sadly missed by Margaret and myself. The gang has broken up and can never be replaced.

May 1966 and I was back at Swan's working on the super tankers. If the Naval Yard had been a poet's dream, then the Wallsend yard was every bit as inspirational. The head piece work counter – Jackie Armstrong – took me under his wing and saw to it that my poems were typed out, photocopied and distributed among the lads. I was tickled pink and I think I was in danger of getting a big head.

All welders were equipped with leather protective gear, gloves, capes and aprons. This gear was forever being damaged in the accident-prone tankers. This was where the 'Leather Queen' stepped in. The Leather Queen was one Lily Groves who sat behind her sewing machine in her little shop beside the tool store and repaired our damaged leatherware. I told myself, 'I must write a few lines about Lily,' and when I did, she was delighted. The poem was framed and hung on the wall of her little workshop. Lily has been a very good friend of mine ever since.

Lily Groves working on her sewing machine at Swan Hunter's.

The Leather Queen

She sits in splendour all alone
Like Cleopatra on her throne
And navigates an old machine
She's Swan and Hunter's 'Leather Queen'.

She'll stitch your glove or mend your cape
Or put your apron back in shape
There is no charge, she sends no bill
If you need gloves, just ask for Lil.

Her place of work is near the store
There's heaps of leather on the floor
And there, amid this busy scene
Is Lily Groves the Leather Queen.

There's always plenty work to do
Repairing old and making new
And welders queue outside her door
From early morn till half past four.

And there behind her bench she sits
And patches aprons, gloves and mitts
She gives you service with a smile
And leather in the latest style.

And when you feel that Winter chill
Do not despair, just go to Lil
And if you're working on the boat
She'll fit you with a leather coat.

And if it ever comes to pass
That we should lose our Leather Lass
You'd see production figures fall
For soon we'd have no gloves at all.

So Swan and Hunter please take note
And listen to this humble poet
If you want progress to be seen
Look after Lil the Leather Queen.

At one time I think I was doing more writing than welding and one day a chap called at my home. He introduced himself as Keith Armstrong, a local writer and publisher, and said that he thought some of my poems were good enough to make up as a small booklet. This was something beyond my wildest dreams, but Keith got to work and he did exactly that. The booklet was only a few coppers but it sold like 'hot cakes', and a few months later we produced a second booklet and I was no longer a secret poet. Suddenly all sorts of wonderful things began to happen. The Shipyard Magazine editor welcomed me to his office with open arms, the BBC took my poem about the 'Million Ton Tanker' and made a cartoon of it for television and Tyne Tees Television did an article about my 'Ghost of No 3'. All this time I was afraid of Radio studios and the thought of appearing on television terrifies me (it still does).

After the giant super tankers and the aircraft carriers, *Illustrious* and *Ark Royal*, were completed the order book started to peter out and gradually the great shipyards of Swan Hunter's were brought to their knees. I applied for my redundancy in 1986 and parted company with a famous shipyard and some very good friends. I am now retired with some very happy memories. The welding stopped but the writing continues.

One day I got a phone call from the popular radio presenter, Frank Wappat, who invited me to come to his studios at North Shields to record a few of my comic poems. I was rigid with fright but Frank dragged me kicking and screaming in front of a mike and after that it wasn't too bad. And now all these years later he often has me on his Sunday afternoon radio programme.

The little colliery village, the Royal Navy and the shipyards seem long ago now, but I remember them all with different degrees of affection. They have all been mentioned in my poems and I hope anyone who happens to read them will find a line or two that may bring a smile to his or her face.

That's all I ask.

The Educated Geordie

There isn't many Geordies
That can taalk as clear as me
It's aal ti' dee wi' voice control
And things like that, you see.

Aa used to hev an accent
And taalked a lot of slang
But elocution lessons
Soon cured my Geordie twang.

And noo my voice is porfect
As nee doot you can tell
Wiv an educated accent
And as clear as any bell.

Aa studied things like diction
And how to shape me mooth
The Missus says Aa taalk just like
The posh folk dee doon Sooth.

Aa've been caalled a gud example
To the bairns alang the way
It's the way Aa soond me vowels you see
The same as Robin Day.

Some think tha A'am an actor
Or a chep from BBC
Aye there isn't many Geordies
That can taalk as clear as me.

You might think that A'am snobbish
Wi' me nose stuck up a height
But you hev to try and look the part
When you're taalkin' aal polite.

Aa lubricate me tonsils
With pints of special Fed.
And Aa practice ivvory morning
When Aa get oot of bed.

Aa've spoke at public meetings
On both sides of the Tyne
And people flock to listen
To this golden voice of mine.

And you'll nivvor find my equal
Nee matter where you gan
Behind this educated accent
Lies a dedicated man.

So if YOU'D like to prosper
And climb the social tree
Take the elocution lessons
And larn ti' taalk, like me.

Jack reading one of his poems.

SECTION TWO

GEORDIE TRADITIONS

Pigeon men show off their birds – and their trophies. A great Geordie tradition.

A Tribute To Wor Jackie

I have stood with sixty thousand
In the wind and snow and rain
I have seen the mighty Magpies
On the wax and on the wane.

I have wondered at the skills
Of Stanley Matthews and the rest
But in my heart of hearts I know
Which one of them was best.

For I remember Milburn
The greatest of them all
The king of all the Geordies
A legend with the ball.

How many times has Jackie
Set St James' Park alight
As he proudly wore the colours
Of the famous Black and White

Yes, I remember Jackie
And his colleagues to a man
How they graced the field at Wembley
And they wrecked the 'Revie Plan'.

A modest man was Jackie
You could pass him in the street
But come kick off on a Saturday
The world was at his feet.

Now who can fill those wing-ed boots
And who can match that pace?
The world without Wor Jackie
Will be a poorer place.

So goodbye Jackie Milburn
You 'Nonpareil' of men
St James' Park will never see
The likes of you again.

Newcastle legend Jackie Milburn runs out onto St James' Park, followed by goalkeeper Ronnie Simpson.

Wor Jackie's statue outside of St James'.

Popular North East pastimes – quoits and whippets.

Geordie The Clubman

Geordie was a club man
A club man through and through
He liked his beer, and he supped his share
Of Federation brew.

Of aall the orly drinkers
George was aalways forst
And the steward said that Geordie
Had the most prodigious thorst.

Geordie was a club man
He nivvor missed a session
To help him pay his drinking debts
His missus took in weshin'.

On Mondays, at the tournaments
He's sup ten pints or mair
And six more on the bus back hyem
And nivvor torn a hair.

Sometimes on a Tuesday
He'd give his wife a treat
And take hor to the 'Bingo'
Making sure she got a seat.

The Bingo started promptly
At twenty five to nine
It was twelve poond if you shouted 'Hoose'
And three poond for a line.

But George preforred a Wednesday
THAT neet the bar was quiet
It gave him time to work upon
His alcoholic diet.

Noo ivvory Thorsday evening
They held a Discotheque
Attended by a thoosand kids
With hair doon past their necks.

But Geordie didn't like it
He said 'They're ower rowdy
And aall that jumping up and doon
'll torn the special cloudy.'

Friday was a sober neet
George only drank two quaarts
That was the neet he took the floor
As Captain of the darts.

His eye was clear, his hoy was strite
When aiming for a double
And them that taalked or made a soond
Would find themselves in trouble.

But Sat'day was the best day
There was nee doot at aall
That was the day when Geordie
Drove his missus 'Up the waall.'

He boozed non-stop, without a break
'til lowse at half-past ten
And then he took twelve bottles hyem
And started off again.

Geordie was a club man
The Club was Geordie's life
And when it came to Sunday neet
He aalways took the wife.

She'd sip a bitter lemon
While George looked on with scorn
And if she wanted mair
She'd hev to pay hor torn.

It was half way through September
When Geordie caught a cowld
He couldn't shake it off at aall
Poor George was getting owld.

The doctor took his temperature
And packed him off to bed
'Just stay there for a day or two
You'll be aalreet,' he said.

But Geordie couldn't rally
And he nivvor eat a bite
He was slowly getting weaker
And he started losing wite.

The Autumn leaves wor faalling
When poor George gave up the fight
And was called before the chairman
Of that Grand Club up-a-hite.

That neet the club was silent
The barmaids shed a tear
The dart team caaled their match off
And they hardly touched their beer.

The chairman caaled a meeting
When he hord of Geordie's deeth
'We must aall attend the funeral
And the Club'll send a wreath.'

They buried George at Benton
(That's just past Forest Hall)
His tombstones there for aall to see
Just by the Chorchyard waall.

And, written on that tombstone
In a hand that's clear and true
Beneath the letter RIP.
Three mair says CIU.

'Cause Geordie was a Club man
A Club man till the end
And when he died that Autumn day
Aall Clubland lost a friend.

But what one lost another gained
'Cause that day in September
The Secretary up-a-hite
Signed on a grand new Member.

All lined up outside their local for a special occasion – perhaps a day trip to Whitley Bay.

Billiards – a popular pastime for many.

The Take Over

This story is a tragic one
That one day may come true
If you're a member of a club
The victim could be you.

The Chairman stood behind the 'Mike'
His face was pale and grim
His hair was combed, his tie was straight
Unusual for him.

The Chairman was a clever man
Advanced in years, but bright
A pint of 'fed' in his left hand
And a woodbine in his right.

He stood before the membership
And sadly shook his head
'We have a problem gentlemen,
And a sticky one,' he said.

'Our little club's in danger
And the reason's plain to see
The women of the district
Are ganging up on me.

They would like to take us over
And form their own committee
And given half a chance, I know
They'll do it, more's the pity.

And if perchance, these women
Should gather in the reins
Then gentlemen prepare yourselves
For further female gains.'

Came the annual elections
And of course the women won
And the management committee
Were toppled one by one.

The secretary trembled
When he heard this latest news
And the chairman of the little club
Was quaking in his shoes.

The redundant club committee
Who'd been slung out on their ear
Had congregated in the bar
And were crying in their beer.

The secretary's face was white
You could tell that he was vexed
He knew his job was on the line
And the chairman's would be next.

And sadly that's what happened
And it wasn't long before
There were no men more in office
And a women on the door.

The members were bewildered
By this 'on the spot' transition
But as the beer remained 'on form'
They accepted the position.

In the midst of all this turmoil
One other thing transpired
In that little mixed up social club
Where the leadership was fired.

On the door was pinned a notice
That was very widely read
It was for the general public
And this is what it said.

'While visitors are welcome
We would like you to remember
Admission is refused to men
Without a lady member.'

The Rise And Fall Of The English Pub

They hung a star above the door
They promised warmth and cheer
A game of darts, a cosy fire
And a glass of honest beer.

And that was how the English pub
Became a way of life
Where tales were spun, and jokes were swapped
And a man could take his wife.

And many merry nights were had
For that's what pubs were for
And everyone paid homage to
The star above the door.

But nothing ever stays the same
At least that's how it seems
Perfection is the kind of stuff
That only lasts in dreams.

The Breweries that owned the pub
(There's none knows how or when)
Were taken over by a group
Of grasping, greedy men.

Throughout the nineteen seventies
Like vultures at a kill
They exploited every avenue
And the public paid the bill.

With every chance, in dribs and drabs
Their prices rose a penny
Their beer became a luxury
And out of reach of many.

Their profits broke all records
As they watched their prices soar
But the public turned in anger
From the star above the door.

Now they're poorer but they're wiser
As they leave their once-loved pub
And they re-direct their footsteps
To their local Social Club.

And each one will be accepted
As a member and a friend
And once more they'll get true value
For each penny that they spend.

May this story be repeated
In each corner of the nation
Down with the greedy breweries
LONG LIVE THE FEDERATION.

The Decline Of The Pint

I'd like you all to stop and think
Especially if you like a drink
Just cast your mind back through the years
Consider how they've changed our beers.

In world war two, and even sooner
Real beer was drank by pint or schooner
Each glass of ale was clear and strong
And every drink was deep and long.

The beer was drawn straight from the wood
No need for stuff like solid food
A man could really quench a thirst
In those days we put first things first.

In private lounge or public bar
We'd stand in line and drain each jar
And volunteers would take the place
Of those who couldn't stay the pace.

This was the school where I was taught
When beer was two and six a quart
Brown Ale was only one and ten
And beer was beer, and men were men.

Those days have gone, alas, for good
We've seen the last of beer from wood
Those happy nights so free from strife
When drinking was a way of life.

The stuff that passes now for ale
Is pressurised and weak and pale
It's stowed in sterile kegs of zinc
A wishy washy fizzy drink.

In ultra modern plastic pubs
And flashy chromium plated clubs
They'll scrape your pockets clean of brass
And fill your jar with froth and gas.

And still they queue to buy this stuff
But as for me, I've had enough
And will I stand around and moan?
Oh no, not me, I'll brew my own.

Cheers! Working men dressed in their 'best' – three piece suits, flat caps and pocket watches.

The Decline Of The 'Stotty Cake'

Oh! crusty golden stotty cake
Just like my mother used to make
In memories I see you still
A'cooling on the window sill.

Round and firm and light of texture
What was that secret stotty mixture
That every mother knew somehow
Oh! stotty cake! Where are you now?

I sometimes walk down memory lane
And live those magic days again
And when I'm there I always take
My fill of mother's stotty cake.

Is there a baker in the land
Who, honestly could turn his hand
To making stotties half as good
As those that my old mother could?

Oh! how I miss you stotty cake
Sometimes I feel my heart will break
Must I be doomed no more to savour
That crispsy crunchy stotty flavour?

But in my mind still firmly placed
Lie memories of that stotty taste
The taste that cannot be forgot
Of stotty cold, and stotty hot.

In canny old 'Newcassel Toon'
They boast about their famous 'Broon'
But every Geordie wil admit
The stotty was the biggest hit.

For they remember long ago
Their mothers making stotty dough
And every Geordie's heart still aches
Remembering those stotty cakes.

But now we must resign ourselves
To buying from the baker's shelves
The product of a lower grade
The stotty now, is 'Tailor Made'.

Fish suppers were the only take-outs for many years. These smart lads and lasses pose outside 'Phillips' Noted Fried Fish & Chip Shop.'

Ode To A Pan Of Broth

Oh Broth, you homely, wholesome brew
No ordinary soup are you
Through Autumn chill and Winter storm
You give me strength and keep me warm.

Who cares if Winter days grow dimmer?
As long as in the pan you simmer
I need no beef or casserole
If you are there to fill the bowl.

Show me a Geordie, if you are able
Who wouldn't leap to join the table
No matter where or what the venue
If you dear Broth were on the menu.

Oh, perfect Broth without a fault
You need no additives or salt
And when December winds are blowing
It's you alone that keeps me going.

Here I sit with spoon and plate
And eagerly anticipate
Fulfillment of my dearest wishes
Oh, Broth you are the King of Dishes.

Steaming in your 'Boody Bowl'
Your sweet aroma stirs my soul
Oh, how can I resist you Broth
You are the candle, I'm the moth.

With you my life will be enriched
Forever I shall be bewitched
Continue then to fill and nourish
Rule on King Broth, long may you flourish.

The Great Willick Rebellion

Forgive me Willick if you can
And as you simmer in the pan
Your sacrifice was not in vain
I only hope you felt no pain.

Inside your twisted shell you lay
Upon the beach at Whitley Bay
While other Willicks swarmed in flocks
At Cullercoats and the table rocks.

All waiting for the likes of me
To pluck you from your friendly sea
Oh Willick is it not a sin
To end up hanging from a pin?

Consider please, the Willick's plight
To you he's just a tasty bite
But somewhere on the ocean bed
Some tears for him are being shed.

For Willicks have their feelings too
And sometimes they can feel quite blue
Especially if their son or daughter
Is languishing in boiling water.

For in these times of grab and greed
When everything is moved at speed
The Willick must accept his fate
For Willicks can't retaliate.

So Willicks of the world unite
The time has come to stand and fight
Now is the time you must begin
Your fight against the dreaded pin.

No longer must you lie and quiver
On ocean bed and mouth of river
And wait until the hand of man
Has placed you in the boiling pan.

So be prepared to shed your blood
And fight the fight for Willickhood
And when your flag has been unfurled
Oh Willick, you can rule the world.

Fish wives selling their wares – including willicks – at the Fisherman's Cottages at Cullercoats in the 1950s.

Poly Donkin – a Cullercoats fishwife.

Bob Johnson's Leek

You'll hev hord aboot the cabbage, that yon chap from Swallwell grew,
How he put his fellow gardeners in the shade.
And it must hev been a wedger, if the tales I've hord are true,
And he must hev been a real clivvor with a spade.

And aal credit to Swallwell, for that greet big cabbage plant,
Though there's some might scoff and say 'it was a freak'.
But I wonder if you've hord aboot the 'pride of Shiremoor',
I mean, of course, Bob Johnson's giant leek.

Now Bob was keen a mustard, when it came to growing leeks,
And his garden was picture to behold.
He'd a sideboard full of trophies, that he'd won at different shows,
And a box of medals made from solid gold.

It was fower in the morning, on July the twenty thord,
When an earthquake tremor wakened Shiremoor.
When they said it was an earthquake, and you know how rumours spread,
But to tell the truth, nobody could be sure.

There were scenes of wild excitement, in the streets that summer morn,
And the shouting could be hord at Whitley Bay.
And a crowd of silly women ran aroon in nighty goons,
Shouting 'Halelujah! It's judgement day.'

The men, of course, were braver, and they organised a sorch,
For to try and find what caused that awful clatter.
When they got to Bobby Johnson's hoose it didn't take them lang
To discover what exactly was the matter.

For there in Bobby's garden, up against the coalhouse wall,
Was the biggest leek that they had ever seed.
The flags were fower yards across, and fifty two feet lang
And still growing at the most alarming speed.

The earth around was heaving, like an ocean in a storm,
And it gave them all a most unpleasant ride.
And it wasn't very funny, when a crack ran doon the street,
And a row of colliery hooses fell inside.

Noo Bob was very sorry, for the damage he had caused,
But there wasn't very much that he could dee.
And the leek just kept on growing for another seven days,
You could spot it twenty miles away at sea.

When the leek had finished growing, and the earth had settled doon,
And the funds to solve their problem had been found.
They got sixty sivven wagons, and a half a mile of rope,
And they pulled the giant leek out of the ground.

An expert from the coalboard came doon to look aroon,
And investigate the newly opened hole.
He descended in a bucket and before he came back up,
He'd discovered fower brand seams of coal.

The leek was cut in slices, by a team of men with saws,
And they worked for just about a week.
And each toon in North East England, got a poss tub full of broth,
All provided by the Shiremoor leek.

Just what he gave his leek to eat, Bob Johnson never said,
But they say he fed it daily from a spoon.
Now he rests in Earsdon Churchyard, and his tomb stone simply says,
'Here lies a man who nearly touched the moon.'

It is quiet now in Shire, but there's some who still grow leeks,
And no doubt they'd like to emulate Bob's feat.
But a leek the size of Bobby's wouldn't have much chance to grow,
'Cos there's no more colliery hooses left to eat.

And that's concludes my story, of the leek that shook the world,
And I divvn't care wherever you may seek.
You will never find a gardener, to tie Bob Johnson's boots,
Or to match his champion Shiremoor leek.

*A proud leek grower with his
prize winning produce.*

The Incomplete Gardener

It happened many years ago
Before my cheeks had lost their glow
And arteries began to harden
My first encounter with a garden.

I still recall the care I took
And how I studied every book
And painfully remember yet
The backache and the taste of sweat.

With garden fork and spade in hand
I savagely attacked the land
And beetles scurried to an' fro
As I applied the rake and hoe.

All day I toiled upon my plot
Removing weed and root and clot
Until at last the job complete
My garden really looked a treat.

Next morning on the stroke of eight
I staggered through the garden gate
Two bags of lime upon my back
And seed potatoes in a sack.

That evening I felt really grand
As I surveyed my plot of land
How set with cabbage, spuds and beet
The finest garden in the street.

I felt so pleased with everything
As happy as the proudest King
I praised the outcome of my labours
And scorned the efforts of my neighbours.

But pride, they say, precedes a fall
True words indeed as I recall
Like figures in a puppet group
My cabbages began to droop.

My raddish and my lettuce seeds
Were smothered in a sea of weeds
My runner beans just wouldn't show
My brussel sprouts refused to grow.

I met my final Waterloo
When all my peas turned navy blue
And tears cascaded down my cheeks
When wireworm attacked my leeks.

I stood amidst my stricken crop
My first attempt had been a flop
And through my tears this vow I made
'I'll never touch another spade.'

I never really got to grips
With Percy Thrower's book of tips
Poor Percy took it on the chin
I threw him in the rubbish bin.

My garden tools were next to go
Out went my spade and rake and hoe
I showed them not one crumb of mercy
Into the bin they followed Percy.

Those days are all behind me now
But I have always kept my vow
My garden stands neglected still
With weeds up past my window sill.

Complaints are tendered by the score
By tradesmen who can't find the door
A postie and a milkman both
Are missing in my undergrowth.

I often sit among my weeds
And think about my wayward seeds
Did they get lost or even worse?
Could they be growing in reverse?

Did I commit some kind of blunder?
And will my crop come up down under?
New Zealand maybe, or Australia?
I'm just a common or garden failure.

Me And My Wellies

There's a hole in the toe of my welly
It's a source of discomfort and pain
It is very unpleasant and smelly
And it lets in the snow and the rain.

And it's not very nice I can tell you
It's a feeling you'll never forget
To have one foot all snug and contended
And the other one sticky and wet.

If you have a nice pair of trainers
Or some comfortable brogues on your feet
I beg you to treat them with kindness
And make sure that both toes are complete.

At functions where dress is informal
I attend with my welly that's holed
With one foot that's perfectly normal
And the other one blue with the cold.

Wellies are very important
Wellies are good for the soul
And I feel very proud of my wellies
Yes, even the one with the hole.

The wife disagrees with my logic
She says, 'Wellies are way out of place
And those who parade them in public
Are nowt but a public disgrace.'

'Get rid of those wellies' she told me
'To flaunt them like this is a sin
They are ragged and tatty and shabby
And the best place for them is the bin.'

Sadly I looked at my wellies
My friends for the last seven years
And I thought of our good times together
Then I choked and my eyes filled with tears.

The wife said, 'I've reached a decision
And here is my verdict,' said she
'In future there's got to be changes
So it's either your wellies or me.'

So I'm holding an auction tomorrow
And I'll smile though my spirits are low
So who wants a fine pair of wellies
One with a hole in the toe.

AROUND TYNESIDE

THE TYNE BRIDGES NEWCASTLE ON TYNE

A view of Newcastle from the air – before redevelopment changed the face of the city centre.

The Geordie Alphabet

A   For the Angel at Gateshead
           The acclaim and the glory are his
           He represents something or other
           But nobody knows what it is.

B   For the buzzer that called me
           In my cap and my tattered old mac
           On my trusty old rusty old push bike
           With me bait in a box on my back.

C   Is for claggy and clarty
           And for chuckin' oot time at the pub
           And for cowpin' yor creels at a party
           An 'C' is for Cullercoats Club.

D   Is for Dut, that's a bowler
           As worn by the toffs of the Toon
           They look very posh and aalways in black
           The American vorsion is broon.

E   Is for Ellington Colliery
           Condemned to be next for the 'heave'
           But the miners were typical Geordies
           They fought and they won a reprieve.

F   For the famous owld Fish Quay
           And the fisher folk doon Borough Bank
           And the Wooden Doll pub on the jetty
           Where many a pint I have sank.

G   For the Geordies in general
           Each one is a good friend of mine
           The salt of the earth are the Geordies
           And they come from both sides of the Tyne.

H   For the annual Hoppins
           And the fun that we have every year
           Exciting but very expensive
           But by hook or by crook Aa'll be there.

I   For the Isle of St Mary
           A magical place for to be
           With its rocks and its pools and its seabirds
           Surrounded sometimes by the sea.

Ellington Colliery before the First World War – now the last deep coal mine in the North East.

Herring boats at North Shields.

An early ride at the famous Hoppins.

The smoke from a paddle ship passes by a sailing ship and St Mary's Island off Whitley Bay.

J   For the jams in the traffic
And the queues that build up at the lights
The bad tempered car driving Geordies
The rows and the brawls and the fights.

K   For the great Kevin Keegan
The man who restored Geordie pride
He rescued Newcastle United
And now they're a Premier side.

L   For the lighthouse at Whitley
On the Island I mentioned before
I thought it was worth one more mention
In fact it is worth three or four.

M   Is of course for the Mackems
The men in the red and white sharts
Sometimes their football is 'Canny'
But Aa'll bet we could beat them at darts.

N   Is for canny Newcassel
The city that we caal the Toon
Noted for Bigg Market parties
And famous for Newcassel Broon.

O   For the owld ootside netty
They've aal disappeared now for the good
Not very hygienic, but handy
Just a hole in a seat made of wood.

P   Is to plodge in the waator
And A'am sure ivorry Geordie agrees
Your enjoyment could not get much better
With your trousers rolled up to your knees.

Q   For the Quayside on Sunday
Where customers surge to and fro
And Geordies arrive by the thoosand
For the great Geordie riverside show.

R   For wor own Geordie Ridley
The famous young Bard of the Tyne
He gave us wor song 'Blaydon Races'
It's wor anthem, it's your song and mine.

S   For the seaside in summer
The crowds and the colliery bands
The pageantry led by the drummer
And the shuggy boats doon on the sands.

T   For the Tyne Tunnel gateway
Just a couple of miles from the mooth
Linking Howden with them gannin' Northwards
And Jarrow with them gannin' Sooth.

U   For the underground stations
On the Metro each side of the line
They're deep and they seem to get deeper
The nearer they get to the Tyne.

V   For the colliery villages
Scattered aal ower the place
They closed doon the mines they relied on
Now they're gone, and left hardly a trace.

W   For Wallsend and Walker
Where Vickers and Swans used to reign
I worked for them both I remember
And I still bear the scars and the pain.

X   Marks the spot for the Geordies
On the map of the land you will find us
On the top right hand corner of England
With the Mackems just one step behind us.

Y   Is for yesterdays Geordies
The folk we remember with pride
We recall them in song and in story
Without them there'd be no Tyneside.

Z   Is the final instalment
You now have it chapter and verse
If the alphabet carried more letters
This poem would even get worse.

A tram passes through a busy Bigg Market. No sign of any of the drinkers it is now famous for.

A packed Newcastle Quayside on a Sunday morning.

Wallsend High Street before the Second World War.

Wallsend Colliery.

The Giant Angel

There's a greet big rusty angel
On a hill in Gateshead Toon
It stands there doing nothing
Just blotting out the moon.

There are some who think it's beautiful
And some who disagree
But the pigeons and the seagulls
Knaa exactly what ti' dee.

The Geordie population
Have been shaken to the core
We've had Roman Waals and Lambton Worms
But nowt like this before.

Noo angels are God's messengers
Aa've aalways understood
They sit on clouds and play their harps
And tell us to be good.

Heaven's full of angels
Superior to man
But is this is what they look like
Aa divvn't want to gan.

Aa've been aroond the world a bit
And seen some funny things
But Aa've nivvor seen an angel
With a pair of oblong wings.

How many years I wonder
Will this angel have to stand
Before it is accepted
As part of Geordieland.

Poets of the future
Will sing the Angel's praises
Men like Geordie Ridley
Who gave us Blaydon Races.

Just a part of Geordie history
Like stotty cake and Broon
And the world will all pay homage
To canny Gateshead Toon.

Memories Of A Colliery Village

Once upon a long ago
Before the Second War
I used to think those distant days
Would last forever more.

I still recall that colliery row
The pit heap at the end
The mining folk I used to know
Each one of them a friend.

The thumping of the poss sticks
In the early morning air
The lines of spotless washing
Some with signs of wear and tear.

The stotty cakes assembled
On the window sills to cool
The tolling of that dreaded bell
That beckoned us to school.

The back shift miner coming
When his stint below was done
The nightshift miner going
Looking sadly at the sun.

The noisy costermongers
And the rumble of their carts
The dirty walk past the houses
And the never ending 'clarts'.

The bosses with their motor cars
I used to watch with awe
The landlord of the Tavern
Standing smugly by the door.

The old men swapping stories
As they passed the time of day
The lamp post on the corner
There the children used to play.

I see again the 'shunters'
On the Backworth Colliery line
And the wagons clanking eastward
To the colliers on the Tyne.

Those days are gone forever
And maybe just as well
For there are other, sadder things
About them I could tell.

Like the rain that fell last summer
On last winter's vanished snow
Enough to say it happened once
Upon a long ago.

A group of men at a Tyneside Colliery before the Second World War. Note some of the men appeare to be soaked.

Times were often hard in the colliery villages of the North East, but there were also many happy days. Here are some images of two special days – the Durham Miners' Gala and the Northumberland Miners' Picnic.

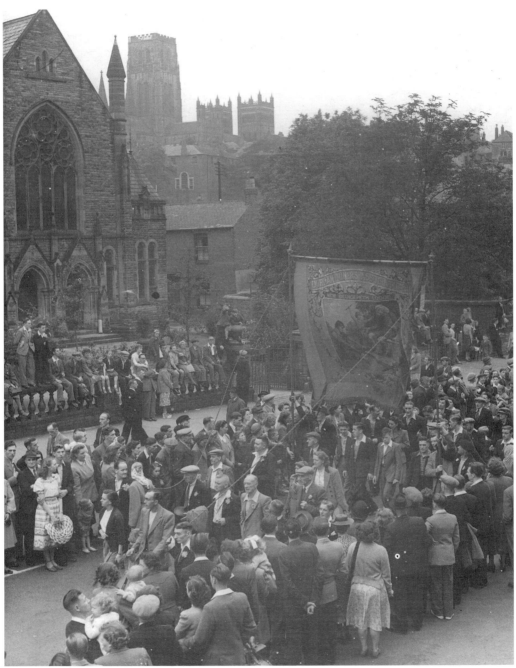

The streets of Durham City is packed for the Miners' Gala in the 1950s.

Marching through Bedlington on Miners' Picnic day in the 1950s. Behind the dignitaries is a Colliery Lodge Banner – one of the symbols of the Great Northern Coalfield.

The colliery beauty queens pass through Bedlington on the day of the Northumberland Miners' Picnic in the 1950s.

A housewife of long ago – knitting at the ready.

The Metro Centre

We went to the Metro Centre
The wife and me that day
We travelled on the Dunston bus
It took wi aal the way.

We crossed the Tyne to Gatesheed
And coined roond ti the right
The bus was full of women
And the sun was shining bright.

The Federation Brewery
Soon quickly came in view
Aa wished Aa could have left the bus
And sampled one or two.

But the wife would have none of it
As the Metro stop drew near
Aa could tell the way she set hor jaw
That today there'd be nee beer.

The bus stopped at the terminus
As buses aalways dee
And we headed for the centre
Aboot fifty wives and me.

We entered Marks and Spencers
Through a big revolving door
Wey Aa've seen some fancy places
But nowt like this 'afore.

It was aal see posh and modern
And ivvorything smelled new
The wife and me felt lost a bit
And she stuck ti me like glue.

Reet through Marks and Spencers
And oot the other side
Then up a moving staircase
And we both enjoyed the ride.

There was potted vegetation
And a kind of balustrade
Aye the Metro shopping centre
Puts the High Street in the shade.

There was plated glass and slidy tiles
And shops too posh to enter
The wife and me felt oot of place
At the Metro shopping centre.

We wandered roond this fairyland
Two strangers lost in heaven
It was two o'clock when we went in
And Aa dragged hor oot at seven.

Back to the bus we made our way
We caught a sixty eight
Aa said 'a pint'll gan doon fine
Before it gets too late.'

'Aa've enjoyed the expidition,'
Said the wife, 'We'll gan back soon.'
Then we nipped across the Tyne
And done wor shopping in the Toon.

Miracle On Tyne

Across the Tyne from bank to bank
From Gateshead to the Quay
A magic bridge has been installed
And it's there for you and me.

We look upon our bridge with pride
And never cease to wonder
How, at the blinking of an eye
Tyne shipping can squeeze under.

And when Summertime gives way
To gloomy Winter nights
The bridge will entertain us all
With merry dancing lights.

The Tyne bridge is a work of art
The Swing Bridge is unique
But the famous Gateshead blinking bridge
Has touched the very peak.

And multitudes will congregate
No need to wonder why
They'll come to see our magical bridge
Our 'Lucy in the sky'.

The New Tyne Bridge. (6th September 1928) 49

The Tyne Bridge shortly after it was opened in 1928.

Swing Bridge (open), Newcastle-on-Tyne.

A tug tows a ship through an open Swing Bridge.

The Wooden Dolly

For many years she stood upon the Fish Quay
A problematic symbol of the past
The figurehead of some forgotten trader
She had travelled many miles before the mast.

And everyone paid homage to the lady
She was worshipped by the sailors' brotherhood
Amazing when you think that she was only
An ordinary Dolly made of wood.

They came from every corner of the nation
Like pilgrims on their journey to a shrine.
And they gathered there in silent acclamation
Round that Dolly on the North side of the Tyne.

Now the Wooden Dolly was famous but unhappy
She was mugged by cruel vandals through the years
They chipped large lumps of wood from off her person
And they carried them away for souvenirs.

As a consequence she started getting thinner
Till the day arrived that everyone had feared
The vandals had removed their final plunder
And the poor old Wooden Doll had disappeared.

The 'Canny folk of Shields' were broken hearted
When the heard about the famous Doll's demise
So they had a 'Whip around' to buy another
On the Quay another Dolly would arise.

A brand new Doll was placed upon the Quayside
On the very spot where once had stood the first
But the 'Canny Folk of Shields' had backed a loser
For once again the vandals did their worst.

Now fishermen have long been known to linger
At the 'Prince of Wales', a pub beside the Quay
And there outside the pub in all her splendour
Is where they planted Dolly number three.

And there for many year she kept her station
She began her stint in eighteen sixty four
Ravaged by the years and local villains
Till a sister Doll took over at the door.

The Doll no longer sands beside the Fish Quay
But she's still around if you would care to look
If you climb up Borough Bank and turn to starboard
You will find her in another, safer nook.

And when you come to Shields please pay a visit
To the library that stands beside the Square
If you look across the road behind the railings
You will see a wooden lady standing there.

And she is proof if ever you should need it
That through the years a legend can survive
For the lady standing there in all her glory
Is the North Shields Wooden Dolly number five.

One of the several Wooden Dollies of North Shields.

Whitley Bay, 1934

Blackpool has its tower
Brighton has its pier
Scarborough has Peasholm Park
And good old Yorkshire beer.

Seaside towns, I love them all
With a fondness tingled with pity
For not a single one of them
Has got a 'Spanish City'.

Except for Whitley Bay, of course
That Northern 'Shangri-La'
Where Geordies came by bus and bike
No one possessed a car.

When I was young, a few years back
My father used to say
'Behave yourself, and wash your face
And we'll go to Whitley Bay.'

Looking back I see myself
Sixpence clutched in hand
Drinking in the wonder
Of that seaside fairyland.

With multi coloured deck chairs
Donkeys on the sands
Music from the carousels
And the local colliery bands.

Candy floss and shuggy boats
And plodgin' in the sea
Yes, Whitley was a magic place
For little lads like me.

All this was many years ago
And things have changed since then
The Whitley Bay I used to know
Will never come again.

The 'Spanish City' still survives
As ageless as the Sphinx
And the early morning Geordie
Still strolls across the Links.

It may be I am getting old
And things are different now
But the magic that was Whitley Bay
Has disappeared somehow.

I know it's wrong for folk like me
To compare now with then
But Whitley was a better place
When I was only ten.

The Shuggy Shortage

On Benidorm the sun is aalways smilin'
The Costa Brava nivvor sees the rain
But when we're on holiday
We gan to Whitley Bay
'Cos there isn't any shuggy boats in Spain.

We've been to Tenerife and Cala Bonna
And we've plodged alang the beach at Cala Dor
But wor pleasure seemed to vanish
For although we love the Spanish
We couldn't find a shuggy on the shore.

It isn't only Spain that has this problem
It's found in other countries big and small
From Majorca to Madeira
Things get dafter, things get queerer
There just isn't any shuggy boats at aal.

If you're off to foreign parts, Aa'd like to warn you
Before you take the plunge and book your flight
If you like a bit of stotty
Whey there's nyen in Lanzarote
And there's not one single shuggy boat in sight.

With aal this new technology advancing
There's nee future for the ordinary man
There's boond to be a scatter
Aa can feel it in me wattor
And the shuggy boats'll be the forst to gan.

Aa've towld the bairns that when it gets to August
Forget aboot the Costa Brava plane
We'll gan to Cullercoats
Where they've still got shuggy boats
'Cos they're ower hard to find in sunny Spain.

Noo Aa wouldn't like to worry anybody
But there's one thing must be clearly understood
We are left with just a few
But the way we're gannin noo
Aal wor shuggy boats will disappear for good.

The Exchange Buildings at Whitley Bay.

On the sands at Whitley Bay before the First World War.

The water ride at the Spanish City.

Enjoying a donkey ride on a local beach.

Elegy On A Colliery Village

In the Kingdom of the Geordies
On the North side of the Tyne
Stood a little colliery village
Just a stone throw from the mine.

It was here I spent my childhood
Underneath a Geordie sky
It was here I learned of laughter
It was here I learned to cry.

I remember Monday mornings
Piles of washing on the floor
When my mother took position
By the poss tub at the door.

A miner's work is heavier
Than most you'd care to name
But the woman at the poss tub
Would put them all to shame.

My memory often takes me
To my colliery home again
And I'm back there in the village square
When I was only ten.

In that little colliery village
In that little colliery street
The lamp post was the centre
Where the children used to meet.

And with undiluted happiness
Beneath the gas light glow
We rode with General Custer
And we fought the Alamo.

The lasses had their 'skippy ropes'
And dolls and 'Hitchie Dobbers'
We lads looked on these things with scorn
We were more for 'Cops and Robbers'.

Money was in short supply
For candy bars and sweets
And excursions to the seaside
Were rare and special treats.

'Money is an evil thing'
The clergymen would say
But folk from colliery villages
Were never 'cursed' that way.

The water taps provided
Were few and far between
And the women battled bravely
To keep their houses clean.

We had no main electric
Or fancy things like that
So they couldn't use a Hoover
To clean the 'Hooky Mat'.

Magic days for children
But not so good for others
Hard work for their fathers
And worry for their mothers.

The village is no longer
Just memories remain
The pit has gone forever
It's passing caused no pain.

There's a modern Supermarket
All posh and very grand
And it's built upon the spot
Where my old village used to stand.

Maybe these busy shoppers
Would stop and say a prayer
If they only knew my village
Was lying under there.

In the Kingdom of the Geordies
On the North side of the Tyne
There used to be a village
And there used to be a mine …

SECTION FOUR

LIFE IN THE YARDS

A welder at Swan Hunter's Shipyard.

A Welder's Dream

I lay that night and counted sheep
And longed for the elusive sleep
Though warm my bed, and pillow light
Uneasy lay my head that night.

Then something very strange occurred
I seemed to fly just like a bird,
And upwards through the starry night
The world below soon fell from sight.

Eventually my flight was ended
And though the clouds I then descended
And there on some celestial star
I found my welders' Shangri-La.

The foremen were extremely kind
And all the counters there were blind
And every job was overhead
No vertical – no flat – no shed.

The gates were always open wide
And those who liked could walk outside
And no one ever barred your way
Or docked the hours from your pay.

With fitted carpets in the tanks
And silver studded staging planks
And hanging in the steering gear
A gold encrusted chandelier.

With air conditioned engine rooms
And both the peaks were free from fumes
The focs'le with upholstered seating
And coffer dams with central heating.

The foremen called each day at three
With coffee, orange juice and tea
And chocolate biscuits 'a la carte'
That's French for 'There's no rush to start'.

Between the berths there could be seen
Sweet scented lawns of velvet green
Along with several other sports
You'd find the welders' tennis courts.
The shoppies were a splendid sight

With golden haloes shining bright
And caring not one single jot
If you're in benefit or not.

A thousand Birds of Paradise
Flew round and made the place look nice
I stood and listened to their song
And that's when everything went wrong.

It wasn't birds that I heard singing
But only my alarm clock ringing
I won't repeat the word I said
When I found I was back in bed.

It's many years since that far night
When I partook in magic flight
But somehow it can never seem
That it was only just a dream.

I don't suppose we'll ever know
What makes imagination grow
Is half our lives a kind of act?
And which half dream – and which half fact?

But some day I will find that star
I'll find my long lost Shangri–La
Up there above the cumulus
I know that heaven waits for us.

Tom McKenzie

Aa remember Tom McKenzie
When we worked for Davy Lamb
We didn't hev much money
And wor bait was bread and jam.

Just two apprentice welders
Two children of the arc
We worked in Waalsend Shipyard
And we played in Waalsend Park.

Dab hands at dodging gaffers
And brewing cans of tea
Aa remember Tom McKenzie
And Tom remembers me.

In the gloomy nineteen forties
When the sirens wailed each night
And wor only smoke was Pasha
And the war was at its height.

Two halfs and ivorry Sunday
We'd work on ship or shed
The homeward through the blackout
Where we'd tumble into bed.

We worked in bad conditions
On galvanise and paint
And in awkward holes and corners
That would aggravate a saint.

But somehow we survived it
And larned wor welding skills
We laughed at life together
And at Hobson and Joe Mills.

Then Tom was made a foreman
Complete with helmet green
He gladly dropped his holder
And he hoyed away his screen.

They gave him fifty welders
Some piece men and some jobbin'
And he led them into action
With cries of 'Screw yor bobbin!'

Young 'uns enjoying a good time around the paddling pool in Wallsend Park in the 1950s – just as Jack and Tom McKenzie had twenty years before.

But now, like many others
He'll soon be on his way
My old mate Tom McKenzie
Is callin' it a day.

The lads are all departing
One by one they go
Like rabbits disappearing
On a Tommy Cooper show.

Aa'll miss you Tom McKenzie
Aa'll miss your smiling face
The yard will be much poorer
When your not roond the place.

But one thing you can bank on
When your clearance notes are signed
And you leave Swan Hunter's
Aa'll not be far behind.

Portrait Of A Foreman

'Father,' said a welder's son
What does a foreman do?
I've seen them strolling round the yard
Do they not work like you?

And who provides the overalls
So smart and neat and green
And how do shipyard foremen
Keep their overalls so clean?

The welder sat and thought awhile
And slowly scratched his head,
'That question is too tough for me
It's got me beat,' he said.

The foremen are the ones my boy
Who get the biggest pay
But what they do to earn it all
I really couldn't say.

From awkward holes and corners
Most foremen claim exemption
This makes for the condition
Of the overalls you mention.

Some are almost human
And some are slightly sour
Some are good and some are bad
And some are drunk with power.

On deck in summer weather
You'll see them at their play
As they gather in their thousands
To pass the time of day.

But when arctic winds are howling
And the worlds in winter's grip
You can spot them on the jetty
But never on the ship.

In central heated offices
They lie among the clover
And venture out at intervals

To kick YOUR fire over.
When things are going smoothly
He's there to take the praise
But hit a snag, and you can bet
He'll disappear for days.

Take notice of your foreman
Heed what he has to say
But when he's gone, just carry on
And do the job YOUR way.

And never try to argue
Don't shout or make a song
Remember he is always right
And you are always wrong.

But some of them are canny
Real gentlemen in green
But sad to say, these ones, my boy
Are few and far between.

Remember what I told you
Learn well what foremen do
For maybe one day you my son
May be a foreman too.

If this should ever happen
Enjoy your share of clover
But don't deteriorate into
A fire kicker-over.

Our Foremen

I've met some foremen in my time
I've seen them fall, I've watched them climb
I've watched them play their power games
And chuckled at their strange nicknames.

There's one who never leaves the job
Rejoices in the name of 'Blob'
There's 'Bootsy', 'Noddy', 'Hoot' and 'Bull'
And one they call the 'Galloping Skull'.

There's 'Poison Dwarf', that wily elf
There's 'Mr Wonderful' himself
Another one you may have heard
Is known to all as 'Whirly Bird'.

With torch and chalk along each seam
The 'Flying Saucer' leads his team
And clustered round each longy butt
The 'Seekers' search for undercut.

Your cup of joy will reach the brim
If you should work for 'Oily Jim'
For though some say he is a cad
He calls each welder 'Bonnie Lad'.

There's one who's never off your back
His name of course is 'Haversack'
There's plenty more, just let me think
Oh yes there's one called 'Panther Pink'.

A little further down the Tyne
There's one called 'PC 49'
And helping him to run the joint
Another one called 'Diamond Point'.

Wallsend Dock have 'Knotty Neck'
And 'Broken Bracket' rules the deck
Across the river they have got
A character called 'Jelly Tot'.

There's one they call 'Four Minute Smile'
He keeps them laughing all the while
That order book and pencil keeper
You've heard about is called the 'Leaper'.

In Smith's of course they have the 'Lung'
The biggest villain yet unhung
And like a 'Baddie' on the telly
A bigger one's called 'Fender Belly'.

At Walker Naval Yard each day
The 'Concorde' swoops upon is prey
And welders flee from 'Whacky Jack'
And wish they had 'Old Tashy' back.

My list, of course, is not complete
There's other names I daren't repeat
And none of them would miss a chance
To lead us all a merry dance.

Before I put my pen away
To every foreman I will say
No matter what you say or do
The lads will stick a name on you.

A bowler-hatted gaffer inspects the work at Swan Hunter's.

Swan's Buzzer

When the hated shipyard buzzer
Splits the early morning sky
Do you ever stop to wonder?
Do you ever reason why?

Do we really need a buzzer?
Do they have them in Japan?
Are they really necessary
For to motivate a man?

It's time a plan was drafted
To ease the situation
And gain a little comfort
For the Wallsend population.

For Wallsend Town is peaceful
The people there are quiet
Why should they be subjected
To this early morning riot?

Swan Hunter we implore you
For everybody's sake
Will you please remove your buzzer
And give the town a break.

We'll manage fine without it
In shipyards and in docks
For most of us have watches
And some of us have clocks.

And if our plea is granted
We'll greet the news with joy
And flock to work in silence
A grateful 'hoi polloi'.

So come on Swan Hunter
And try to act the toff
Please think about your neighbours
And switch that buzzer off.

Drama At The Gate

To some it seemed a stroke of luck
That morning when the gate got stuck
And men of every trade and rank.
Were stranded on the shipyard bank.

The gateman – poor unhappy soul
Stood sweating by the gate control
And in a state of nervous fever
Manipulated gate and lever.

And though he pushed with might and main
His efforts proved to be in vain
For just as though it bore a grudge
The stupid gate refused to budge.

And adding to the gateman's worries
A growing fleet of motor lorries
In single file like ships of state
Advanced upon the stubborn gate.

A manager appeared – and then
Addressing all the locked out men
He told them 'with a little luck'
He'd quickly get the gate unstuck.

'But should I fail to get you in'
He told them with a crafty grin
'I have a clever plan in store
I'll lead you through the foremen's door.'

But Morris (he's the shipyard cop)
Raised up his hand and shouted 'stop'
No ordinary working mortals
May enter through these sacred portals.

The pointers now were touching ten
And still the bank was black with men
But here and there a few had been
Escaping from the crowded scene.

How long the crowd would stick together
Depended more or less on whether
The gate was opened up before
The Penny Wet unlocked their door.

The entrance to Swan Hunter's Wallsend Shipyard.

A brace of navvies armed with picks
On loan from Brims for twelve and six
Declared that first thing after bait
They'd tunnel underneath the gate.

And fifteen minutes past the hour
They plied their picks with skill and power
But six feet down I must explain
The navvies struck a water main.

A tidal wave of H_2O
In breadth and depth began to grow
It battered down the gatehouse door
And swept poor Morris off the floor.

Down past the shed our bold Gendarme
With butterfly and over-arm
Made records set in Mexico
Appear to be extremely slow.

A forward roll without a fault
A backward double somersault
He finished with a belly flop
And landed in the plumbers' shop.

But meanwhile what about the gate?
How feared the men who had to wait?
Read on my friend and soon you'll know
You haven't very far to go.

A plater's helper found the trouble
He thought that he was seeing double
For wedged beneath the gate there lay
A large unopened welder's pay.

They quickly got the lifting gear
To lift the heavy packet clear
And with the utmost care and speed
The shipyard gate was duly freed.

Thanks to the trouble at the gate
The day shift started three hours late
And this (as Tom McIver stated)
Would never more be tolerated.

While Morris, who had braved the storm
Was drying out his uniform
McIver planned a big surprise
To cut the welders down to size.

His scheme turned out to be a winner
It made the welders' wages thinner
His guile was clearly demonstrated
He had their price list terminated.

'The reason,' said he with a grin
'If I can make their packets thin
By placing them upon a rate
Their wages cannot jam the gate.'

And this is how they fixed the gate
That Autumn day in sixty-eight
And why welders of the Tyne
Now stand upon the hunger line.

Dark Deeds In The Shed

They found the nightshift foreman
In a corner of the shed
He was very stiff, and very cold
And very, very dead

He lay between a transverse
And a section of the deck
And an iron powder welding rod
Was wrapped around his neck.

The body was discovered
By a plater and his mate
They decided to report it
But first, they'd have their bait.

Because, bait is most important
When you're working in the shed
And a foreman doesn't matter much
Especially if he's dead.

A 'butcher' from the ambulance room
Arrived upon the scene
As the foreman lay there silent
In his suit of Lincoln green.

He took the nightshift foreman's pulse
Then, as his brow he mopped
He said, 'This man is either dead
Or else my watch has stopped.'

Then in came Albert Walker
A scowl upon his face
He said, 'We can't have foremen
Lying dead around the place.

So take off that transverse
And get him out of sight
There's plenty other foremen
I'll send you one tonight.'

The news reached Frankie Thompson
And Charlie Humble too
And they quickly hurried shedwards
To see what they could do.

Frank gazed upon the foreman
As he lay upon the deck
And he ordered the removal
Of the rod from round his neck.

'These rods are too expensive
To waste like this,' he said
And he gave it to a welder
Who was working in the shed.

The Tyne Tees Television
Sent down two camera crews
And they interviewed a sergeant
Who was looking round for clues.

The sergeant faced the cameras
And waved his stripes around
And, in his poshest voice, he said
'This bounder must be found.

It's not so much the foreman
He's easy to replace
But iron powder welding rods
Cost thirty bob a case.'

They took the night shift foreman
To the place where foremen go
It's a kind of foremen's scrapyard
Where it is I do not know.

And the shed resumed production
In that old Swan Hunter style
Albert Walker lost his scowl
And someone claimed they saw him smile.

On the notice board next morning
This message could be read
It was mainly for the nightshift
And this is what it said.

'On account of recent trouble
In the Wallsend Shipyard (East)
And regarding damaged welding rods
And a foreman now deceased.

The management would like to say
To all the nightshift squads
Please try to be more careful
With your iron powder rods.

And if you hate your foreman
We know just how you feel
But, if you want to strangle him
Please, do it with mild steel.'

The Mauretania – launched by Swan Hunter's in 1906 – was one of the greatest ships ever built on Tyneside. Here are three images of its construction.

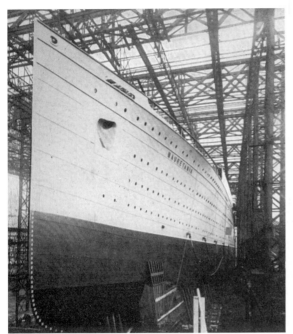

The massive turbines of the Mauretania at the Wallsend Slipway and Engineering Company.

The Titan Crane lifts a boiler on board the Mauretania.

The Admiral's Visit

There were groups of shipyard managers
Assembled here and there
And a host of supervisor types
Were dashing everywhere
There were flags above the gatehouse
And the guards stood to attention
With the medals on their uniforms
Too numerous to mention.

The scrubbing brush battalion
Had been toiling overnight
The cranes were painted yellow
And the staging painted white
Two hundred surplus welders
Were lined up on parade
For the Admiral was coming
An impression must be made.

So they dusted all the 'Shoppies'
And they stood them in a row
At the bottom of the gangway
Where the Admiral would go
They whitewashed all the bollards
And the stones along the jetty
And they utilised two Union Jacks
To hide the workmen's netty.

The pointers of the shipyard clock
Were touching half past eight
When a fleet of stately limousines
Came gliding through the gate
Inside the leading motor car
The Admiral reclined
A happy and contented man
Just freshly wined and dined.

There were scenes of great excitement
In the Wallsend yard that day
And the cheering of the workers
Could be heard at Whitley Bay
The women cleaners curtsied
Each worker doffed his cap
And a band of shipyard managers
Were even heard to clap.

As the Admiral alighted
From his gleaming limousine
He commented to his chauffeur
That the yard was nice and clean
He nodded with approval
To the management and men
Then he jumped back in his motor car
And drove away again.

So the Admiral departed
And his cortege followed on
And the yard got back to normal
When the Admiral had gone
The 'Shoppies' were collected
And put back into their box
And the bunting was dismantled
From the ship upon the stocks.

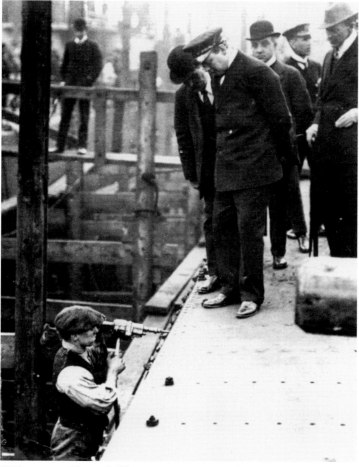

Winston Churchill visits a Tyneside shipyard.

The managers retired
To the managers' 'Retreat'
For an early cup of coffee
And perhaps a bite to eat
The foreman did what foremen do
Whatever that may be
And the crowd of surplus welders
Wore put back into their cree.

And that is how it happened
On that gloomy Winter day
And why everything is painted
From Carrville to Benton Way
There are some who'd quickly criticise
Swan Hunter's tired men
But it only needs an Admiral
To wake them up again.

A ship is launched – a time of great celebration. At one time this was a common sight on the Rivers of the Tyne and Wear.

Big Norman's Shoes

The headlines in the Daily News
Were all about big Norman's shoes
One was split, the tongues too short
The other had a list to port.

The Daily Mirror stated too
That Norman's shoes just wouldn't do
They said, 'We must proceed with haste
To see that they are both replaced.'

Sid Bell could not oblige at all
The shoes in stock were much too small
For Norman's feet, (to put it mild)
Would drive the bravest cobbler wild.

The local shops were just as bad
They couldn't help the giant lad
So Swan's committee met that day
To see if THEY could find a way.

They sat and talked the clock around
But no solution could be found
Until, at last they formed a plan
That satisfied them to a man.

In Clelland's Yard, next day at nine
Two keels were laid beside the Tyne
Two keels that really made the news
These were the start of Norman's shoes.

Six platers and a burner too
Were put to work on either shoe
With seven cobblers from the dole
To stitch the uppers to the sole.

Three welders toiled inside each toe
Two on top and one below
And these received the highest pay
For they were claiming CSA.

The tongues were lifted into place
And neatly tacked along the base
Each lined with seven yards of crepe
The shoes at last were taking shape.

A squad of shipwrights made the heels
And, placing them on bogie wheels
With skilful and exact precision
Manoeuvred them into position.

The lace holes rings were fitted then
By special lace hole fitting men
Inserted through the outer cases
While Haggies worked upon the laces.

The giant shoes were now complete
And ready for big Norman's feet
Just when the job seemed in the bag
That's when they struck a major snag

They stood in splendour side by side
Two shoes to fill the heart with pride
A credit to the builders ... BUT
BOTH MADE TO FIT BIG NORM'S LEFT FOOT.

Hood Haggies Works, Willington Quay. (No. 106)

Haggies Rope Works at Willington Quay.

Ten men were sacked, and over night
The foreman plater's hair turned white
And, on the stroke of nine o'clock
The management resigned en bloc.

On June the tenth at ten o'clock
They towed one shoe to Palmer's dock
And there they toiled by day and night
To change that shoe from left to right.

And poor old Norman waits and hopes
His old shoes fastened on with ropes
But confident that soon he'll wear
A brand new made to measure pair.

If you're a cobbler, don't delay
Report to Palmer's right away
Help make the big lad's joy complete
And get him back upon his feet.

It was once the biggest crane in the world – at North East Marine Engineering Company at Wallsend – it would have come in handy to lift Big Norman's shoes.

The Welders' Football Match

Yes, I can still remember when
The Foreman Welders played the men
And though it lays no claim to fame
It was the most amazing game.

Spectators came from near and far
They came by bus and private car
They came a thousand voices strong
To cheer their favourite team along.

Jack Armstrong was the Referee
A stern unbiased man was he
With whistle, pencil, watch – the lot
He stood upon the centre spot.

The Linesman were the strongest pair
And both looked rather worse for wear
One waved his flag in drunken frolic
The other was an alcoholic.

Excitement touched a fever pitch
With tempers poor and language rich
At last onto the field of play
The Gladiators made their way.

The Foremen wearing fearsome frowns
Led by their Captain, Billy Downes,
In strips of scarlet edged with white
Were really quite a splendid sight.

The Welders on the other hand
A quiet unassuming band
Ran out in strips of faded green
Behind their Skipper, Willy Keen.

A coin was tossed and there and then
The Welders' ranks were cut to ten
For, (as the doctor later said),
The penny fell on Willy's head.

Two stretcher men without delay
Took Willy off the field of play
And so before they kicked a ball
The Welders' backs were to the wall.

The whistle blew, the game began
The Welders' lines were over ran
A shot for goal by Thirlaway
Tore half the centre stand away.

A skilful move by Walter Taylor
He dribbled round old Reggie Naylor
From thirty yards he had a crack
And knocked the Ref upon his back.

By then the Welder had a try
And down the wing was seen to fly
Determined to find fame and glory
The Centre Forward, Ronnie Storey.

He bobbled and weaved along the line
Fast making ground and doing fine
And piercing their defensive wall
If only he had had the ball.

Then reappearing on the scene
With bandaged head came Willy Keen
One shoulder charge from Downes – and then
They carried Willy off again.

A fine display of soccer skills
By wing men Lackenby and Mills
That body swerve of Jimmy Gent
And that was how the first half went.

The half time whistle blew at last
And Ronnie Elsdon – working fast
Presented to each sweating Gaffer
A juicy, yellow, king size Jaffa.

The second half – and yet again
The Welders only fielded ten
The Foremen struck with head and boot
Refreshed, no doubt by Ronnie's fruit.

The ball ran out to Tommy Mac
Who sold a dummy to the back
A crafty flick, a forward nod
Onto the toe of Charlie Bod.

Now this was Charlie's chance of fame
One kick and he could win the game
But circumstances alter cases
You see he hadn't tied his laces.

Just like a super sonic jet
His boot flew in the Welders' net
Confusion reigned around the goal
When Charlie Body lost his sole.

The game resumed and still no score
But none could guess what lay in store
For as the cheers and singing rang
The ball exploded with a bang.

The Referee appealed for calm
And using all his tact and charm
He said, 'No harm's been done at all
Just send us out another ball.'

A top Official blushing red
Ran on the playing field and said
'I'm sorry Ref, it can't be done
We haven't got another one.'

A hundred Groundsmen ran around
But nowhere could a ball be found
From Walkerville to Forest Hall
They searched but couldn't find a ball.

As evening shadows ended play
The Referee abandoned play
And arguments rang long and loud
From both the players and the crowd.

The Welders nursed their aching joints
And claimed that they had won the points
They pointed out that they had been
Without their Captain – Willy Keen.

The Foremen disagreed and cried
That they were much the better side
At least they scored a kind of goal
If only with a Flying Sole.

It's many years since that affray
That goalless draw with no replay
The players now are past their best
Their football boots are laid to rest.

But better men I've never seen
Those twenty one plus Willy Keen
A goalless draw but all the same
It was the most amazing game.

The Clearance Sale

The berths were standing empty
The river clear of ships
There was talk of unemployment
On everybody's lips.

The caulkers had been silenced
Snuffed out the welder's flash
The workers' hands were empty
And short of ready cash.

No more the buzzer sounded
In the early morning chill
The steward of the Social Club
Stood by an empty till.

Hard times once more were with us
The days ahead looked bleak
And Swan Hunter's workers
Were truly up the creek.

Some drastic steps were needed
Agreed the shipyard bosses
Some plan of action must be found
To help them cut their losses.

And that was how it started
A plan that must not fail
They all agreed the answer was
A bargain clearance sale

The shipyard gates next morning
Were opened wide to all
And bargains by the thousand, lay
Against the shipyard wall.

Welding rods a penny each
And windy pipes a tanner
Nuts and bolts a bob a bag
And free with every spanner.

Wing bulkheads, ten shillings
Complete with staging brackets
And from the fab shed very cheap
Ten dozen welder's crackets.

Boilersuits and helmets
All sizes strong and light
Unused to work and good as new
Of course they're all in white.

And if you'd like a garage
Or a large unfurnished flat
Nip down to Swan's and if you're quick
They'll sell you Trevor's hat.

There's a thousand acre Fab Shed
With a buzzer on the top
There are cranes of all description
And a complete joiners' shop.

A super tanker rudder
Is going very cheap
Just place it on your sideboard
It's guaranteed to keep.

A forepeak or a coffer dam
Will set you back a fiver
To purchase both of these, you'll need
A note from Tom McIver.

If you can't find a bargain
Among this shipyard stock
Come back next Monday morning
They're clearing out the dock.

A ship is launched from Swan Hunter's before the First World War.

The Welder's Lament

You may think I'm in the pink
But my stomach's full of zinc
And the shadows on my lungs are getting bigger
With my head inside a mask
I will tackle any task
I've been told that I cut quite a dashing figure.

Yes I really think I'm grand
With my holder in my hand
I am king of all the workers on the boat
And it's me you have to thank
For the fumes inside your tank
And the holes that you find burning in your coat.

You can see me every morn
Looking rather pale and worn
In my hand a pint of milk is firmly held
Though a wreck is what I am
I don't give a Coffer Dam
And I still contrive to fiddle while I weld.

My hair is getting thin
And my lungs are caving in
And my eyes are not as keen as they might be
Several pints of Exhibition
Would improve my poor condition
And I think the firm should give it to me free.

We're a special kind of men
You will see us now and then
On a weekend, and we almost pass for toffs
But take notice for a while
And you'll see somebody smile
And say they're welders I can tell them by their coughs.

When my time on earth is done
And I've scaled my final run
And I stand before Saint Peter's gates of gold
Step inside my boy he'll say
Throw that mask and milk away
The first welder, with the cheek to join my fold.

My Kind Of Shipyard

If we could start at nine o'clock
Instead of half past seven
Then Wighams would be paradise
And Swan's a bit of heaven.

If Monday was a day of rest
And Friday, double time
And three weeks holiday every month
Then life would be sublime.

If managers would play the game
And look the other way
Our tea breaks would last longer
And there'd be more time for play.

And 'late arrivers' at the yard
Would much appreciate
If someone in authority
Would scrap the shipyard gate.

In Summer, when the tanks are warm
And minutes seem like hours
We'd like a workers' swimming pool
And how about cold showers?

When snow and frost festoon the decks
Like icing on a cake
Then here's a small suggestion
That I would like to make.

If Alec Marsh could find the time
To open up the store
We'd pile in every winter
And stay until the thaw.

We'll have, (If these things come to pass)
Much shorter, brighter days
Just one big happy family
All pulling different ways.

SECTION FIVE

THE PENSIONER'S LAMENT

The Pensioner's Lament

My hand is not so steady now
The eye is not so bright
My hair is past redemption
And the bit that's left is white.

The feet are not so nimble
The spring no longer there
And my teeth in quick succession
Are following my hair.

Sometimes when I'm shaving
I see visions of my youth
But it's only wishful thinking
And the mirror tells the truth.

Look not at me with pity
My friend, for if you do
You might see someone somewhere
Looking similarly at you.

There are none of us improving
And the sands of time run fast
God made us all to flourish
But none of us to last.

So throw away your troubles
Enjoy yourself today
Tomorrow is tomorrow
And a thousand miles away.

So fill your glass and raise it
And drink a toast with me
To all the happy days to come
And to the days that used to be.

The sparkle might be fading
And my hair fast getting thinner
But the teeth I have remaining
Could wreck a navvie's dinner.

And so I count my blessings
One two three four five
I haven't very many
Still it's good to be alive.

I have my share of worries
And more debts than you could mention
But I'll be out tomorrow
With my buss pass and my pension.

The Incomplete Motorist

There's a battered Mini Morris
On the street outside the door
If you want it, you can have it
I don't need it any more.

I bought it from a dealer
Back in nineteen sixty two
At the time it seemed a bargain
Though the tax was overdue.

The steering wheel was fractured
The roof was sprouting grass
The windscreen, (in a dreadful state)
Was made of frosted glass.

There were tadpoles in the battery
The hooter wouldn't hoot
And some nocturnal vandal
Had spent a penny in the boot.

The floor was made from sections
Of a shipyard staging plank
And the gear box was adapted
From a second world war tank.

The ancient braking system
Was all faith and hope and trust
And a geriatric engine
Lay beneath a coat of rust.

On examining the tyres
I found one of them was sound
But I must admit, the two front wheels
Were not exactly round.

When I tried to get it started
It remained as dead as mutton
And a swarm of bees flew out the dash
When I pulled the starter button.

Next day I got it started
Midst clouds of steam and smoke
It was thanks to four star petrol
And an engine on full choke.

The neighbours lined the pavement
And raised a mighty cheer
I was doing seven miles per hour
Flat out in second gear.

As I struggled with the steering
And I tried to keep my head
I approached a busy crossing
With the traffic lights on red.

The brakes just wouldn't hold her
So biting back a curse
I slammed my foot down on the clutch
And put her in reverse.

What happened next, you wouldn't believe
I suffered fifty frights
The boot went back to where we'd been
And the engine jumped the lights.

Next day before the magistrates
I stood the legal ground
The charge was careless driving
The fine was fifty pounds.

A poorer but wiser man
I suffered for my blunder
No money left, and even worse
My Mini torn asunder.

The car was in a dreadful state
With roof and floor entangled
The starboard side was inside out
The port side badly mangled.

I towed both halves to Clelland's
They specialised in Minis
They quickly knocked her into shape
The fee was seven guineas.

And that battered Mini Morris
Still stands outside my door
If you want it, you can have it
I don't need it any more.

It's had two previous owners
As far as I can tell
They've got them in a mental home
They share a padded cell.

The Incomplete Window Cleaner

I always do the best I can
To help about the house
I'll tackle any job at all
To please my loving spouse.

I have failed at paperhanging
I just couldn't make the grade
And my efforts in the kitchen
Were disastrous I'm afraid.

My knowledge of electronics
And hoovering machines
Or keeping gardens tidy
Was way beyond my means.

But I was always willing
You can be sure of that
So I thought I'd clean the windows
And earn my back a pat.

Step ladders and a bucket
A leather and a duster
And a king size box of 'Daz'
Was all the tools that I could muster.

I applied them with great gusto
I was really very keen
But there's more to cleaning windows
Than I thought there would have been.

You may think there's nothing to it
If YOUR windows need a wipe
But it's tricky on a ladder
If you're not the ladder type.

My pride was badly dented
My dignity was stung
When I tried to climb that ladder
And I missed the second rung.

I was lying at the bottom
With the bucket on my head
When I heard the neighbours laughing
I wished that I was dead.

My window cleaning future
Faced uncertainty and doubts
As I lay there semi-conscious
In my patch of Brussel sprouts.

Removing the appendage
I pulled myself together
And I searched around the garden
For my duster and my leather.

My composure now returning
And my tools once more complete
I reluctantly decided
That I must concede defeat.

Cleaning windows is for people
More adept than me at climbing
And it seems there's something lacking
With my balance and my timing.

So I handed in my bucket
With the windows still unwashed
With my ego slightly dented
But far from being squashed.

I have skills as yet uncharted
Though admittedly erratic
And next Saturday, I've promised
I will insulate the attic.

The Incomplete Housekeeper

The wife was sick, confined to bed
'She needs a rest,' the doctor said
And there for seven weeks she lay
While I could only wait and pray.

And meantime much against my wishes
I learned the art of washing dishes
And how to dust and scrub and rinse
The memory still makes me wince.

Now cooking grub may seem to you
A very simple thing to do
But if you've never cooked before
Then stay outside the kitchen door.

I still remember how I tried
To make myself a plate of fried
I thought 'How simple women's games'
That's when the pan went up in flames.

I learned the lesson there and then
The frying pan is not for men
The kitchen is a woman's realm
A woman's hand should guide the helm.

I stood before my stricken pan
A sad and disillusioned man
My confidence was badly shaken
As I surveyed my cindered bacon.

And so to put it plain and blunt
My efforts on the cooking front
Had been a failure from the start
That wayward fry up broke my heart.

What happened next, as I recall
Completely drove me up the wall
The pungent smell of burning metal
Was coming from the kitchen kettle.

Held in the grip of black despair
I sank into the kitchen chair
My fry up in the rubbish bin
And a kettle with no bottom in.

That's when my wife came into view
As wives are always wont to do
And although sick and quite unable
Soon had a meal upon the table.

She's better now, back on her feet
My cup of joy's once more complete
And life resumes that 'Rosy glow'
I'm back again to 'Status Quo'.

The nightmare is behind me now
No furrows linger on my brow
I leave the cooking to my spouse
I'm just the 'Man about the house'.

As for my culinary skill
next time the wife is taken ill
I'll fortify my lonely days
By eating Chinese take aways.

And when my spell on earth's done
And Heaven's fortunes have been won
I hope the angel at the gate
Will volunteer to make my bait.

A local shop from before the days of the supermarket —showing of its goods and its well dressed staff.

The Incomplete Shopper

I must have looked a proper wally
Parading with my shopping trolley
Dodging weaving left and right
And flapping like a paper kite.

I must have covered many miles
Up and down these shopping aisles
Trying hard with main and might
To keep the little wife in sight.

Past the ham and potted meat
Then three times round the shredded wheat
A picture of complete dejection
Proceeding in the wrong direction.

It's not a joke (to put it mild)
To have a trolley running wild
Just scraping past each market shelf
Pursued by someone like myself.

Two hundred shoppers turned and fled
As I approached the crusty bread
And panic spread along my route
Through kiddies' wear and frozen fruit.

My journey reached a sad conclusion
When in the general confusion
The trolley did a figure eight
And crashed into the check-out gate.

The manager came into view
And said, 'I want a word with you
Somewhere there'll be another store
That will appreciate you more.

I have this glut of damaged stock
My staff is suffering from shock
And furthermore to put it plain
My trolleys cannot stand the strain.'

That's when the wife came into sight
Apologising left and right
Accusing me of indiscretion
And ruining her shopping session.

My trolley days are over now
And things are not the same somehow
When I approach a superstore
They won't allow through the door.

Barred from every store in town
But I won't let them get me down
I try to lead a normal life
And do my best to help the wife.

And when the larder's getting low
Out with my shopping bag I go
No manager can make me stop
You'll find me in the corner shop.

Jack and Margaret on holiday.

The Incomplete Decorator

'This house needs decorating,'
The missus said to me
'The paper in the living room
Is hanging off,' said she.

The staircase is disgraceful
And all the paint is peeling
There are cracks upon the kitchen walls
And patches on the ceiling.

The time has come to waken
From your life of indecision
There's more to life than drinking beer
And watching television.

The power of a woman's tongue
Is very hard to beat
As usual she won the day
And drove me to my feet.

Next day the scene was altered
I showed her who was the boss
Instead of watching telly
I watched a tin of gloss.

I was balanced on a ladder
With a bucket full of paste
And a yard of Anaglypta
Was entangled round my waist.

When I stumbled on the landing
It just added to my cares
When a stream of white emulsion
Went cascading down the stairs.

The wife, to put it mildly
Was not amused at all
And she didn't much appreciate
The skid marks on the wall.

Or the splashes on the carpet
Where the ceiling paint had dripped
Or the spots upon the window
Where my painting brush had slipped.

And she wasn't very happy
With the bedrooms back and front
For the paper fitted badly
And the scissors had been blunt.

The boot marks on the wardrobe
Really made the missus squirm
And the thumb holes in the paper
Where my grip had been too firm.

I stood amid the wreckage
And surveyed the disarray
And I came to the decision
That this was not my day.

Dexterity and artistry
Are qualities I lack
Maybe that's the reason
Why the wife gave me the sack.

I sit behind my tankard
And smile into my beer
The wife has taken over
The way ahead is clear.

In future I'll be missing
When the ceiling starts to crack
And the paintwork starts to crumble
In the bedroom front and back.

You will find me in the local
With both elbows on the table
Just a no good decorator
Very willing, but unable.

The Morning I Fused The Light

No words among my repertoire
Could soothe the pain or heal the scar
Or dim the memory of my plight
That morning when I fused the light.

The morning air was chill and damp
And I was left without a lamp
I blindly groped across the floor
And stubbed my toe against the door.

No time had I to nurse my bruise
No time to mend that wayward fuse
Around the clock the pointers raced
I must be off to work in haste.

A candle helped relieve the gloom
And shed some light around the room
I found my cap and boilersuit
Then snapped the lace that tied my boot.

Then came the thing I feared the most
The dreaded smell of burning toast
I must have looked a sorry sight
That morning when I fused the light.

A cup of tea I quickly grabbed
As from my eye a tear I dabbed
Then feeling almost fit and able
I knocked the milk jug off the table.

I left the house in deep despair
Into the soggy morning air
Behind me things were in a muddle
That's when I stepped into a puddle.

I hobbled through the driving rain
I missed the bus and lost the train
And loudly cursing luck and fate
Arrived at work an hour late.

The foreman in a fit of rage
Demanded forfeit from my wage
He quickly learned I was annoyed
That's how I joined the unemployed.

So now I'm just an also ran
A sadder but a wiser man
But one thing I will tell you plain
I'll never fuse the light again.

The Tablets

Aa take twenty sivvin different kinds of tablets
Aa get them from the NHS for nowt
The pink ones are for diarrhoea and sickness
The yellow ones for duzzy boots and gout.

Aa take tablets for to wake me in the morning
And tablets for to help me sleep at night
Aa take tablets for aal kinds of other problems
Like gainin' too much fat, and losin' wite.

The doctor said me health would get much better
With more exercise and less time in the club
And the reason for my sad degeneration
Is too much baccy, too much beer, and too much grub.

'Remember son that you are only human
And the human frame can only stand so much
Take my advice, forget about the smoking
And kick the drinking habit into touch.'

Sound advice but difficult to follow
Especially by a hopeless case like me
But you should aalways listen to your doctor
Of this A'am sure that you will aal agree.

Aa've done me best to follow his instructions
By cuttin' doon on drink and smokin' less
But self control gave rise to other problems
And noo A'am takin' tablets for stress.

Food For Thought

In supermarkets everywhere
Some customers are in despair
And I have seen plain signs of panic
When they have heard the word 'Organic'.

We're entering a brand new era
And foodstuff could be getting dearer
The scientists have made an error
And that's the reason for this terror.

The aggravation caused by them
Combined with letters G and M
Prepared the ground for future wars
On shop and supermarket floors.

Apples growing on the tree
Look very nice to you and me
But who can tell? We have no guide
And maybe they've been modified.

The humble turnip is in doubt
And can we trust a Brussels sprout
Is the little garden pea
All that it's cracked up to be?

With thoughts too horrible to mention
I view each meal with apprehension
These doubts are ganging up on me
And I am in a quandary.

Now when I see the table spread
I scrutinise each course with dread
Is there some hidden fiend who waits
To spring upon me from the plates?

We the public must awaken
And measures must be quickly taken
It's time somebody caused a fuss
Before the food starts eating us.

Going Metric

What happened to the hundredweight?
What happened to the pound?
Has the little ounce gone missing?
Is the bushel still around?

Twelve inches used to make a foot
And three feet made a yard
All simple English measurements
And held in high regard.

A metre can be used I know
By builder and surveyor
But I always thought a kilogram
Was a kind of record player.

The normal British working man
Enjoys a pint of ale
Some drink it by the schooner
Some drink it by the pail.

But what lies in the future
For the poor old drinking classes?
I've heard some nasty rumours
That they're planning smaller glasses.

When we've all gone continental
And the Euro's have their say
It looks as though the poor old pint
Will soon be on its way.

We'll become a metric nation
Ruled by the number 10
We'll be little metric women
And little metric men.

When our future has been cobbled
And we've all survived the fright
And we've gone all European
And we're driving on the right.

Then, when the dust has settled
There'll be time for you and me
To look back with affection
To the days that used to be.

The Holidaymaker

I've never had a holiday
I've never been to Spain
I've never crossed the ocean
By liner or by plane.

I've never been to Paris
I've never been to Rome
The only holiday I've had
Are holidays at home.

Maybe come next Summer
I'll get some cash together
And travel to some distant land
In search of better weather.

I'd like to go to Scarborough
Blackpool is too far
But the bus fare is expensive
And I can't afford a car.

Perhaps a cycling holiday
Is something I would like
But one big snag arises
I cannot ride a bike.

Fortune is a fickle thing
I'll wait for mine to alter
And then I'll join those happy crowds
At Benidorm and Malta.

Every dog must have his day
And mine will come I know
And when it does, my bags are packed
I'm ready for to go.

But miracles don't happen
At least they don't for me
Holidays are hard to get
They never come for free.

So I'm saving all my coppers
I keep them in a jar
With all this wealth behind me
Next year I'll travel far.

Endowed with all these riches
My cares will fly away
And I'll holiday at Cullercoats
Or even Whitley Bay.

Failure On The Fells

For holidays or summer breaks
They told me I should try the Lakes
And all my cares would disappear
When I discovered Windermere.

The sun was shining that July
When off we went, the wife and I
We left behind the shipyard smells
And headed for those magic Fells.

On reaching there, we quickly spied
A camping spot at Ambleside
The perfect spot, no argument
So that is where we pitched our tent.

And in that flimsy canvas shell
We slept beneath a Lakeland Fell
Completely unaware that we
Were heading for calamity.

Monday morning lay ahead
The tent was warm, as was the bed
But as the pointers turned to six
The weather started playing tricks.

I crept out of the tent that morn
To face a doubtful Lakeland dawn
The prospect didn't look too good
I was kneeling in a sea of mud.

The biggest cloud I ever saw
Was crawling down the hill next door
A massive wave of H_2O
Swept down that hill on us below.

Like a thousand horses on the hoof
The raindrops battered on the roof
We clung together in our tent
And that is how the Monday went.

Tuesday's dawn broke dull and grey
It seemed more rain was on the way
And come it did, I won't forget
Our camping clothes got soaking wet.

Wednesday and Thursday came
And the weather still remained the same
By Friday things had got no better
And Saturday was even wetter.

On Sunday I was spitting blood
When the tent collapsed into the mud
The time had come, we both agreed
To flee the Lakes with utmost speed.

Now we are home, the wife and I
Our camping clothes are almost dry
We left our tent behind for good
It lies beneath the Lakeland mud.

My admiration knows no bounds
For those who brave these camping grounds
My wife and I now somewhat shyer
Would really favour somewhere drier.

Next time we go on holiday
We'll turn our face the other way
We'll leave behind the clouds and rain
And pitch our tent in sunny Spain.

A picture postcard of Ambleside.

The Bandit

He stands there in the corner
A villain plain to see
Extracting money right and left
From folk like you and me.

Club members queue before him.
With money clutched in hand
And thought they like to curse him
He's always in demand.

The club committee love him
They tend his every need
If he should fail in any way
They'll put him right with speed.

What is the strange attraction
This villain seems to hold?
And why do people flock to him
Surrendering their gold?

His hunger's never satisfied
And money is his grub
He's rightly named the 'Bandit'
There's one in every club.

He stands there in his corner
And does his daily stint
While sneering at the multitude
That he has rendered skint.

If you should ever meet him
Don't give in to temptation
If you resist the Bandit
You can buy more Federation.

I do not like the Bandit
He is no friend of mine
If we should never meet again
Then that will suit me fine.

But somehow I can't help it
I've always liked a bet
Just one more brief encounter
And I'll drop that jackpot yet.

The Mobile Phone

If I could get a tax-free loan
I'd buy myself a mobile phone
And join the ultra modern crowd
With conversation long and loud.

On busy bus and crowded train
I'd view my neighbours with disdain
There's no way they could vie with me
I'd have a mobile phone you see.

In public places with my friends
My vanity would know no ends
And life would be extremely sweet
Just striking poses in the street.

Though I'm a non-religious type
I'd think maybe the time was ripe
So every night I'd kneel and pray
A mobile phone would come my way.

But prayers are a last resort
Vain pleading to a higher court
Someone up there would smell a rat
And mobile phones don't come like that.

In every street my friends still stand
With mobile phones clutched in their hand
All looking down their nose at me
With smug superiority.

But one day they may fall from grace
And proudly I will take their place
And have a mobile of my own
If I can get a tax-free loan.

Remember Tommy Atkins

He stands there sad and silent
A soldier made of stone
He used to march with thousands
But now he stands alone.

The open sky above him
The busy street beneath
And around him lie remnants
Of last November's wreath.

He represents the heroes
Of world wars one and two
Who gave their lives unselfishly
And they died for me and you.

The tear drops are less frequent now
As memories recede
The busy world just hurries by
And no one seems to heed.

Yes, memory can falter
And recollection fade
But the debt we owe that soldier
Can never be repaid.

They call him Tommy Atkins
He laid no claims to fame
He looked just like the boy next door
But a hero just the same.

In Flanders Field he took the blows
The heartache and the pain
And Tommy Atkins played his part
Once more at Alamein.

The years roll by and still he stands
A symbol of the past
But, come what may, I pray to God
His memory will last.

My story is a simple one
But every word is true
Remember Tommy Atkins
And what he did for you.

Men of the Northumberland Fusiliers who had taken part in a Sergeants' rifle competition.

Happiness

If you should ask in times of stress
What is this thing called happiness?
Elusive as the rainbows end?
I'll tell you what it is my friend.

Happiness is Friday night
A five pound note, a shirt that's white
A glass of ale, a cigarette
A corner seat, a winning bet.

A dream of wealth and high finance
First 'divi' on the treble chance
Both elbows on the public bar
The last instalment on your car.

A day without a drop of rain
A holiday in sunny Spain
A double top, a prial of Kings
Yes, happiness is many things.

It's ham and eggs at half past eight
Away from dock and shipyard gate
It's country air, it's new mown hay
It's watching children at their play.

For some it means a new Rolls Royce
For others, Julie Andrews' voice
It goes with Canterbury lamb
It's even in a jar of jam.

It's roses blooming in the park
It's Piccadilly after dark
It's cheering an Olympic runner
It's Swan and Hunter's million tonner.

It's everything you wish yourself
A favourite book upon the shelf
A carol sung on Christmas night
A Christmas tree by candlelight.

It lies to North and South and East
It comes to those who search the least
If you should find some, please take care
There isn't very much to spare.

Yesterday

The years stretch out behind me
And clearly I can see
A small boy in the distance
A boy that once was me.

I live again those magic days
Re-calling everything
Like tadpoles in a jamjar
And conkers on a string.

Tops and whips and skippy ropes
And home made paper kites
I remember how I savoured
Those after school delights.

Apprenticed to the game of life
I still had much to learn
Like climbing trees, and skinning knees
And fishing in the burn.

Regardless of the weather
In snow or wind or rain
There were footballs to be kicked about
And marbles in the lane.

Sometimes in the evening
I switch off my TV
And those happy days of long ago
Come flooding back to me.

Once again I join the gang
And every day is Spring
With my tadpoles in a jamjar
And my conkers on a string.

Glossary Of Terms

For non Geordies – and those who did not work in the shipyards – here are explanations for some of the terms used in Jack's poems.

Geordie Expressions

Bait – packed lunch or sandwiches.
Claggy and clarty – sticky and dirty.
Cowpin yor creels – turning somersaults.
Crackets – small stools on which one could sit rather than having to kneel when welding low positioned jobs.
Hitchie dobbers – Smooth round piece of material, usually a jamjar bottom or a round tin can lid, used in the children's game of street bays.
Hookey mat – Home made mats made by working class women – some of them almost works of art.
Hoppins – Annual Town Moor Fair.
Lowse – knocking off time, time to go home.
Mackems – Sunderland folk.
Netty – toilet.
Plodge in the waator – paddle in the sea.
Shuggy boat – a boat-shaped swing found on the beach.

Shipyard Terms and Characters

CSA – nothing to do with erring fathers, it simply means 'Confined space allowance'.
Coffer dam – two watertight bulkheads, standing a few feet from each other forming a watertight barrier.
Peaks – the extreme fore and after ends of a ship.
Screw yer bobbin – Tom McKenzie, a popular foreman welder, used to urge his men to work with cries of 'screw yer bobbin'. What this meant, only Tom MacKenzie knew.
Trevor's Hat – a popular foreman plater who took a lot of good natured ribbing about the size of his green safety helmet.
Charlie Humble – shipwights' manager.
Tom McIver – a very powerful director and was second in command to Sir John Hunter, who was the biggest wheel of them all.
Morris – uniformed guardian of the Wallsend shipyard gate, affectionately known as 'Morris the poliss'.
Frankie Thompson – a manager, head of the plating section.
Albert Walker – a very stern shipyard manager, never known to smile.

Miscellaneous

Pasha – an evil smelling wartime cigarette.
Revie Plan – Manchester City's star player when they faced Newcastle in the 1955 Cup Final was Don Revie. Their system of play – based around the forward – was know as the 'Revie Plan'.

List of Poems

THE PEOPLE'S HISTORY

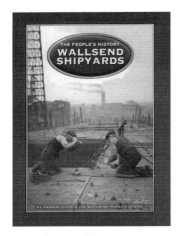

THE PEOPLE'S HISTORY
WALLSEND
SHIPYARDS

BY ANDREW CLARK & THE WALLSEND PEOPLE'S CENTRE

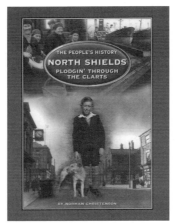

THE PEOPLE'S HISTORY
NORTH SHIELDS
PLODGIN' THROUGH
THE CLARTS

BY NORMAN CHRISTENSON

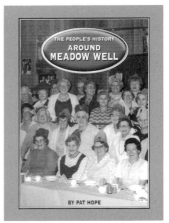

THE PEOPLE'S HISTORY
AROUND
MEADOW WELL

BY PAT HOPE

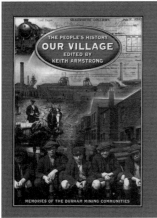

THE PEOPLE'S HISTORY
OUR VILLAGE
EDITED BY
KEITH ARMSTRONG

MEMORIES OF THE DURHAM MINING COMMUNITIES

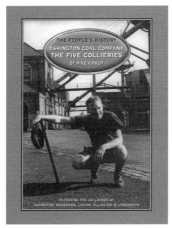

THE PEOPLE'S HISTORY
ASHINGTON COAL COMPANY
THE FIVE COLLIERIES
BY MIKE KIRKUP

FEATURING THE COLLIERIES OF:
ASHINGTON, WOODHORN, LINTON, ELLINGTON & LYNEMOUTH

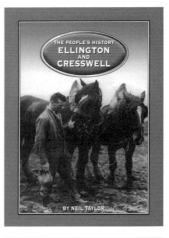

THE PEOPLE'S HISTORY
ELLINGTON
AND
CRESSWELL

BY NEIL TAYLOR

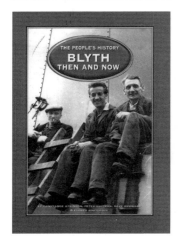

THE PEOPLE'S HISTORY
BLYTH
THEN AND NOW

BY CONSTANCE ATKINSON, PETER HUTTERS, DAVE GURMAN
& A LEWIS MONTGOMERY

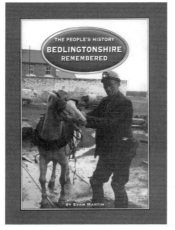

THE PEOPLE'S HISTORY
BEDLINGTONSHIRE
REMEMBERED

BY EVAN MARTIN

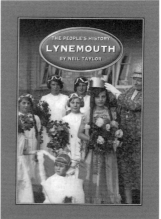

THE PEOPLE'S HISTORY
LYNEMOUTH
BY NEIL TAYLOR

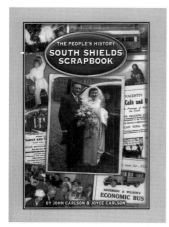

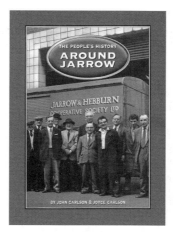

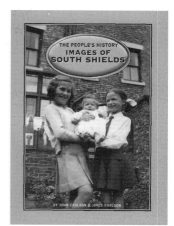

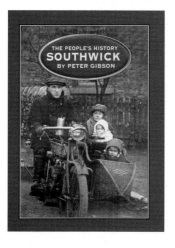

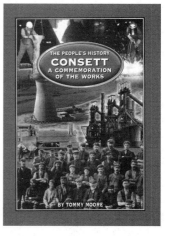

Also available: Charlie Crowe's Newcastle United Scrapbook ... Cop On The Tyne ... Chirton And Percy Main ... Glimpses Of Old South Shields ... Memories Of Bedlingtonshire And Beyond

The world famous Tyne Bridge with four other bridges in the background – High Level, Swing and the Railway.

The People's History

To order a book in The People's History series send
a cheque or postal order to:

The People's History
Suite 1
Byron House
Seaham Grange Business Park
Seaham
County Durham
SR7 0PY

All books are £9.99 and postage and packaging is free.

Cheques and postal orders made payable to The People's History Ltd.